Bird Cherry
Roshni Gallagher

VERVE
POETRY PRESS
BIRMINGHAM

PUBLISHED BY VERVE POETRY PRESS
https://vervepoetrypress.com
mail@vervepoetrypress.com

FIRST PUBLISHED FEB 2023

Printed and bound in the UK
by Imprint Digital, Exeter

ISBN: 978-1-913917-30-2

CONTENTS

Bird Cherry

April River

That morning I said *too much* –
it felt like stumbling out into the garden at night

and plunging right into the pond.
Later, *too much* followed us out on the drive

and out through the fields. Followed whilst the heat
made moons of our upturned faces –

as the clouds dandelioned apart.
I wanted to unloosen into the ice

of the April river. I wanted to be a gill.
The water was clear and cold and quiet.

Its depth a boulder against my belly.
My eyes still sticky with pollen.

In the river I found every river
I'd ever touched. Meadowsweet

and wet trouser cuffs.
I wanted to be cleansed. Like blooming silt,

like water over rock. Instead,
the river dappled and deepened its mirror

and I met myself – unchanged.

The Whitby

The moon is thin and poised like a curlew's beak –
all bone. Hanging over the ocean, the abbey.
We watch the sea birds being swept by the wind
and I try to tell you about all my life you've missed.
There are still so many sentences I can't reach.

I know that out on the water, welcomed home,
is a replica of the ship they took my ancestors in –
to sugar plantations for former slave owners.
The Whitby, sailing from India to the Caribbean,
a stale silence blowing in off the water to greet her.

Coming back here is like mutely looking down
on my own odd body as it moves without me.
Nothing is familiar. This loved, blank cliff
is a memorial stone with the names bleached out.

My Head is Full of Goat

My head is full of goat
and of other looping things.

I sit in the blue rolling shade
of the trees and the cool air on my face
makes it feel like I'm neck deep
in the sea.

The day the goats broke loose
it rained so hard
waves swept down the street.

Why does naming something
seem to make it true
as though it hadn't been before?

In my mind I watch the goats trot by
again and again –

they raise a racket
their tough little hooves striking stone
beneath the water.

Isn't it enough to say
that I'm wading through the world
and I'm soaked to the bone?

Whale Song
Edinburgh & Strandhill, North Atlantic Ocean

On my phone I read that today the water is 5°C. I imagine the sea is white froth, black, indigo.
Below and far away the quick heartbeat calls of minke whales –
the groan and chirp of humpbacks.

In my mind's eye I'm always standing in the same two places –
up to my knees in seawater or pulling up a chair at the kitchen table.

When I spend so long thinking of the ocean the hum of traffic starts to sound like whale song.

Parting

I watched the moon rise
and the moon rise
catching planes to Ireland,
just in time
to find you alive

for a minute,
and later at the church no one knew
how I was related to you.
Your secular, brown grandchild.

You should have died a day earlier,
they said,
you must have been holding on
for the last one
to arrive.

When the priest came knocking

for the third time we shut him out
and he stood for a moment clutching
his beads in the rectangular window
of the hospice door – *The line between*
comedy and grief really is that thin –
someone knew there wasn't time
for another rosary because suddenly
we're watching the life tip gently
out of her

        like water from a cup
and we all lean inward as though
to catch some part of her leaving or as
though we're pulled forward the equal
and opposite reaction to her slipping
away so when you cough and say *now*
then trying to shake off the feeling like
a dog shivering off water I'm glad,
for a moment, to be taken briskly outside
so that we might go to an art gallery
or a book shop or a café down by the river
somewhere with books and a fire
but I'm thinking *what are we doing*
your mum has just died, all this before
I learn what a wake is and before
I mumble my first hail marys *and why*
are there so many and before I'm the only
brown person at the funeral and you're

smiling and trying to usher me through
the art gallery gates as though this were
an interruption in my yearly visit to Sligo
and now that the worst has happened
and the waiting is over with what's left to do
but mother me.

Yesterday's Snow

Crammond beach, North Sea

On new year's day, two days after my granny's funeral,
I run into the water.
The waves bite my ankles.

On my hands and knees I scour the shore for sea glass

Sea colours   loam, olive, lotus leaf, kelp, cola.
A honeyed wolf moon.   A blood orange periwinkle.

The sea breathes softly.
I imagine yesterday's snow   melting silently into the waves.

Swimming Pool With a Glass Roof

My arms look darker,
against the whiteness of the still water,
than I thought.

The white moon
observes me
behind the glass.

One day,
I will own a kitchen table.

There'll be brown faces,
and brown faces
that I just haven't met yet

and I'll bring them bunches of pink flowers so dark and full
they will flow and roll off the surfaces
and their brightness will cause the air to stir.

For now whiteness and reflections
of me and moon,
dissolving.

Dock Leaves

Often, I want to flick shut
strangers' eyelids.

I'm sick of anticipating my own othering.
Thank god for places where people aren't –

the green of the trees has always been a door
to walk through and become whole.
The green sinks into me and the woods beat

with spires of dock leaves,
deep red, like a hundred bold hearts.

Who dared trick me
into thinking I was a guest?
up ahead, the wild silver lake exists

for a brown girl
to crouch beside it and try to catch the frogs.

I've Been Hiding

The ridge of the fish bone
mountain rises in air out of my dreams.

Sand dunes fall
in the grey stacked roof of the city.

The light shifts and catches
the bright belly of a gull. I've been hiding –

out in the hush and howl.
Deep in the splintering sea.

My Granny Dreams of Guyana

My granny looks at me and she sees herself.

Her living room full of glasses, half drunk.
Pictures of gods hang above the bed. She listens

to a record spinning out in another room,
                another house.

                The rant of rain on begonias.
                Mangrove and wood slats. The parrot's asleep.

Things change.
I try to pull quiet in to cover us.
                The walls sing.

She looks at me
and she sees herself
                in the slant moon,
                the water,
                the waning bank.

Attend

You sit outside language now
& I think of everything unsaid –

your brink　　& beating tide
the lilac of your mornings.

I know you in fragments –

Your Capuchin
Sheep　Parrot　Pelican –

                                        they didn't have names!

I frame your photo
attend you
                from a distance.

Imagine　orange
flowers wilting　in the heat
at your mother's
unattended funeral.

                        I couldn't go back for hers
                so I wouldn't go back for anyone else's.

Wear black
when I learn your Indian name,
light incense,
        let you be whole with your secrets.

                                That's Roshni, isn't it?

In the silence

I hold a nib of your life's words

& claim   &   claim.

Ache
Mullaghmore beach, North Atlantic Ocean

As a child I thought I was a dolphin

                  that could leap over the waves

                                  cold white foam on my shoulders

my eyes on the horizon

                       my ears beneath the water

the click   crackle   creak

             of bubbles

                           the ache of the sea

washed up on the shore

                I lie quietly on the sand like a cuttlefish bone

In my first memory of us

I'm nervous you'll be eaten
by a paper spider hung
above the classroom door.
With oil pastels, I drew us
both as smiley white girls
under big orange leaves.
Mum still has that drawing
hung up on her wall –
me the mirror of you.
Remember when you fell
and cut your knees into two red
circles and I couldn't stop crying?

Bird Cherry

To teach myself belonging.
I try to find the name
of the blossom tree darkening
by the window.
Bird cherry or sweet cherry –
from the curve of its leaves
I hold each possibility of its ungrown
berries in my mind.

If I met my great-great grandmother
I wouldn't know the name
of the language she spoke.
Bird cherry or sweet cherry.
In the dusk, the petals fall in drifts
like sea foam.
The soil remembers
everything it used to be –
carbon, fracture, petal.
Last month, the full white blossoms
swelled and blotted out the sky.

I Only See Deer With You

I only see deer, she said, *with you.*
As we picked our way around nettles,
the brambles snagging at our ankles
and our pockets heavy with acorns,
and anything else October offered us.
'Til we reached the hollow in the woods
where the earth caves in,
as though some small meteor once hit –
the trees have grown crookedly around it
and filled the space with orange leaves,
and we came across a deer
standing stock-still in the sinking gloom.
Her eyes staring back at us like wild stars –
the first to rise in the night.

When You Called Out My Name

Because of you, I twist my cauliflower in turmeric.
Because of you and your declarative love –
of fat aubergines steeped in miso,
and for slowly fried tofu, crisp shining chilies.

I coat every white nook until it's bright brown.
Brown women taught me how to love myself by loving.
When you called out my name in the street last week
it sounded like depth. Like roots stirring.
Like a summoning within myself.

From the kitchen I look out at the bare trees
and there, perched alone, is a brown breasted Sparrowhawk
held completely in the branches like she never had to arrive.

I think of the newly full tree.
The striking fullness of your heart naming mine.

All at Once

Last night I found you –
walking through my dreams.

Your voice was light unravelling
down the stairs.

A string of pearls –
all at once –

> I remembered
> & you remembered me.

On the floorboards the sun
pooled into a seed.

Your house was bright
with sleep.

It was you
it was you.

> I remembered.
> You came back for me.

NOTES & ACKNOWLEDGEMENTS

In 'The Whitby', the boat referenced in Whitby harbour is the *Endeavour*.

I'd like to thank the editors of the following journals/anthologies where some of these poems have previously appeared: *Best Scottish Poems, Butcher's Dog, Gutter, Interpret, Lunate, Middleground, New Writing Scotland, Our Time is a Garden* published by the Institute for Advanced Studies in the Humanities, *Propel, the Scotsman, Scottish BPOC Writer's Network Audio Anthology.*

Thank you to my writing communities for the years/days/hours spent writing together, for being my first readers and editors, and for pushing me to become a poet: everyone at the Scottish BPOC Writer's Network, my fellow writers at Nomad Magazine, and the writers and poets with Our Time is a Garden. Thank you to all the poets whose workshops and editorial advice have inspired and shaped these poems.

Thank you to the Edwin Morgan Trust and all the 2022 Judges for awarding poems in this pamphlet an Edwin Morgan Poetry Award and thank you to the Scottish Book Trust for awarding me a New Writer's Award - these resources have helped me to create this pamphlet.

Thank you to my wonderful writing mentor Nadine Aisha Jassat for pushing me to dream bigger for myself and nurturing my poetry practice.

Thank you to Stuart at Verve Poetry Press for giving this quiet collection of poems a home.

Thank you to my parents, Kathleen and Derek, and my wonderful family for creating a world for me where poetry was always valued - I'm very lucky! Thank you to my friends for all the love and support you've shown me and my poetry.

Finally, thank you to Fergus and our cat, García, for filling every day with love.

ABOUT THE AUTHOR

Roshni Gallagher is a poet from Leeds living in Edinburgh. She is a winner of the Edwin Morgan Poetry Award 2022 and the Scottish Book Trust's New Writers Award 2022. Her work has appeared in a variety of literary publications including *Best Scottish Poems, Gutter, New Writing Scotland*, and *Propel*. In her work, she explores themes of nature, connection, and memory. Find her on twitter and instagram: @roshnigallagher or at roshnigallagher.com

ABOUT VERVE POETRY PRESS

Verve Poetry Press is a quite new and already award-winning press
that focussed initially on meeting a local need in Birmingham - a need
for the vibrant poetry scene here in Brum to find a way to present
itself to the poetry world via publication. Co-founded by Stuart
Bartholomew and Amerah Saleh, it now publishes poets from all
corners of the UK and beyond - poets that speak to the city's varied
and energetic qualities and will contribute to its many poetic stories.

Added to this is a colourful pamphlet series, many featuring poets
who have performed at our sister festival - and a poetry show series
which captures the magic of longer poetry performance pieces by
festival alumni such as Polarbear, Matt Abbott and Genevieve Carver.

*The press has been voted Most Innovative Publisher at the Saboteur Awards,
and has won the Publisher's Award for Poetry Pamphlets at the Michael Marks
Awards.*

Like the festival, we strive to think about poetry in inclusive ways and
embrace the multiplicity of approaches towards this glorious art.

https://vervepoetrypress.com
@VervePoetryPres
mail@vervepoetrypress.com